大展好書　好書大展

品嘗好書　冠群可期

大展好書　好書大展
品嘗好書　冠群可期

彩色圖解
太極武術
21

嫡傳楊家太極拳
——精練28式

Authentic yangfamily tai chi quan 28 form

中國武術八段

傅聲遠 著

大展出版社有限公司

國家圖書館出版品預行編目資料

嫡傳楊家太極拳——精練28式＝Authentic yangfamily tai chi quan
28 form／傅聲遠　著
——初版，——臺北市，大展，2007〔民96・11〕
面；21公分，——（彩色圖解太極武術；21）
ISBN　978－957－468－568－4（平裝）
1.太極拳
528.972　　　　　　　　　　　96017576

嫡傳楊家太極拳——精練28式

著　　者／傅聲遠
責任編輯／佟　　暉
發 行 人／蔡森明
出 版 者／大展出版社有限公司
社　　址／台北市北投區（石牌）致遠一路2段12巷1號
電　　話／（02）28236031・28236033・28233123
傳　　眞／（02）28272069
郵政劃撥／01669551
網　　址／www.dah-jaan.com.tw
E - mail／service@dah-jaan.com.tw
登 記 證／局版臺業字第2171號
承 印 者／傳興印刷有限公司
裝　　訂／建鑫裝訂有限公司
排 版 者／弘益電腦排版有限公司
授 權 者／北京體育大學出版社
初版1刷／2007年（民96年）11月
ISBN　978－957－468－568－4　　　　　定　價／220元

楊家太極拳祖師　楊祿禪
（1799 年～1872 年）
Master of Yang Style Taijiquan (shadow boxing)
Yang Lu Chan

楊鳳侯（祿禪公　長子）
Yang Feng Hou

楊班侯（祿禪公　次子）
Yang Ban Hou

楊健侯（祿禪公　三子）
Yang jian Hou

楊少侯（健侯公　長子）
Yang Shao Hou

楊澄甫（健侯公　三子）
Yang Cheng Fu

楊兆元（健侯公　次子）
Yang Zhao Yuan

楊兆林（鳳侯公　子）
Yang Zhao Lin

楊兆鵬（班侯公　子）
Yang Zhao Peng

傅鍾文（兆元公　外孫婿）
Fu Zhong Wen

傅宗元（鍾文公　胞弟）
Fu Zong Yuan

傅聲遠（傅鍾文之子）
中國武術八段
楊式太極拳親族傳人
世界永年太極拳聯盟主席

Fu Sheng Yuan
（The Son of Fu Zhong Wen）
Chinese Wushu level 8
Cognation descendant of
Yang Style Taijiquan

傅清泉（傅聲遠之子）
中國武術七段
楊式太極拳親族傳人
世界永年太極拳聯盟副主席

Fu Qing Quan
（The Son of Fu Sheng Yuan）
Chinese Wushu level 7
Cognation descendant of Yang
Style Taijiquan

楊澄甫老師與弟子傅鍾文
Master Yang Chengfu and disciple
Fu Zhongwen

楊澄甫老師與弟子傅鍾文在廣州
Master Yang Chengfu and disciple
Fu Zhongwen in Guangzhou

1932年傅鍾文跟隨老師楊澄甫到廣州市政府教拳
Fu Zhongwen and his master Yang Chengfu taught Taijiquan at
Government of Guangzhou City in 1932

傅鍾文　Fu Zhong Wen

傅聲遠和師伯崔毅士（中）、
牛春明（右）老師在上海
Fu Shengyuan and his senior
master Cui Yishi, master Niu
Chunming at Shanghai

傅鍾文與傅聲遠推手
Tuishou between Fu Zhongwen and Fu Shengyuan

澳大利亞總理霍克親切會見傅氏父子
Australian Prime Minister Mr. Bob Hawk gave an interview to father and son of Fu

中華全國體育總會顧問徐才與傅聲遠合影
Group photo of Xu Cai, adviser of Chinese Sport Association, and Fu Shengyuan

傅鍾文墓園
Fu Zhongwen's
Cemetery

傅公紀念祠大殿
Palatial Hall of Master Fu
Zhongwen's Memorial
Temple

傅公鍾文銅像
Bronze of Master Fu Zhongwen's Memorial Temple

傅聲遠被授予中國武術八段
Fu Shengyuan is awarded
Chinese Wushu level 8

傅聲遠和西班牙政府官員合影
Group photo of Fu Shengyuan
and officer of Spanish

傅聲遠和西班牙學生
Fu shengyuan and Spain
students

10

傅聲遠和葡萄牙學生
Fu Shengyuan and Poutugal students

傅聲遠和泰國學生
Fu Shengyuan and his students in Thailand

傅聲遠和德國學生
Fu Shengyuan and his students in Germany

傅聲遠和美國學生
Fu Shengyuan and his
students in America

傅聲遠和英國學生
Fu Shengyuan and his
students in England

傅聲遠和智利學生
Fu Shengyuan and his
students in Chile

傅聲遠和阿根廷學生
Fu Shengyuan and his
students in Argentina

目　錄

高歌武術文化

徐　才

　　12 年前，聲遠先生所著《嫡傳永年楊式太極拳》面市時，我曾於他寫過一篇短序《將武術獻給世界》以示祝賀。兩年前國際武術聯合會隨著武術在世界蓬勃發展之勢，決定每年 5 月爲「世界太極拳月」。今年在這個「世界太極拳月」裡，聲遠先生傳出喜訊，他又有幾本新書即將付梓，並再邀我爲之作序。我深爲這位移民海外的中華赤子之心所感動，所以接受了這項囑托。

　　我首先要向已是 76 歲高齡的聲選先生致敬：您眞老當益壯，老有所爲。從您的作爲又能看到您教子有方，代代相傳祖業的心路。眞是上天不負苦心人。傳鍾文、傳聲遠、傳清泉太極世家三代人，定當一代勝似一代。

　　20 年前，聲遠先生懷著把太極拳弘揚海外的虔誠之心移民澳洲。時間催人老，也催人的事業興。聲遠到了澳洲不顧年齡增長奮力進取，把太極拳這個中華武術的品牌在四十多個國家傳播得風風火火，他以澳洲爲立足點，每年教遊四方。這正如美國著名的未來學家奈斯比特（John Naisbitt）在《亞洲大趨勢》書中所說：「西方正在學習適應東方化，而澳洲則首當其衝。」聲遠先生在海外傳拳授拳，就像他的父親傳鍾文大師那樣，不只是傳技而且傳理，還要傳德。這「三傳」是聲遠先生執教之道，也是他爲人師品。我衷心祝願海內外熱心傳播中華武術的朋友，在「三傳」上狠下功夫，努力把中華武技、武理、武德廣泛撒播人世間。

聲遠先生在海外授拳創業，20年可謂成績斐然。這些年他勇於探索，勤於筆耕，以圖書和影帶形式向海內外習武者貢獻了太極拳的文化財富。在多元化的當今世界，不同文化的交流與交融是個大趨勢。不久前我從報紙上讀到一篇文章說：「與中國對外貿易『出超』相比，中國的對外文化交流和傳播則是嚴重『入超』，存在『文化赤字』。」這個論斷引起我強烈共鳴。是啊！中國是具有五千年歷史的文明古國，有著十分豐富的文化遺產，如今中國人民又在創造著嶄新的文化財富。爲什麼在文化「出口」方面我們處在一種弱勢狀態呢？這恐怕與我們對固有的文化強勢認識不足，對人類文化的互相凝聚，彼此滲透認識不足有關。

這裡說一個至今仍然能鼓舞國人奮力傳播中華文化的一位先輩人士，他就是清末在西方世界彌漫著歧視中國、歧視中華文化的氛圍下，率先以流暢的法文撰寫《中國人自畫像》、《中國人的快樂》、《中國戲劇》等書，向世界介紹中國和中華文化的陳季同。陳季同是福建人，他與同屬閩籍的辜鴻銘、林語堂是近代中國人用西文向世界介紹中國和中華文化的「福建三傑」。他們的作爲對當今盛世中國的文人武士具有莫大的啓示意義。可喜的是在中華武術走向世界的潮流中，已經出現一批以精湛的拳術和深情的筆墨向世界展示武術風采的專家，聲遠先生就是其中之一。我深切期望海內外武術家攜手高歌武術文化，造福於人類的健康、益智、修性，共創和諧社會和和諧世界！

2006 年 5 月於北京

太極拳説十要
Yang Cheng Fu's Ten Important Points For Practic

楊澄甫

一、虛靈頂勁
Hold the Head straight with Ease

頂勁者，頭容正直，神貫於頂也。不可用力，用力則項強，氣血不能流通，須有虛靈自然之意。非有虛靈頂勁，則精神不能提起也。

The head should be erect in order for the spirit to rise. If force is used, the back of the neck will be stiff, and the circulation of blood and chi will be impeded. There should be a natural, light and sensitive feel-ing. If not, the spirit will be unable to rise up.

In order to achieve the above, it is important that the neck is held straight, but very relaxed and alive. Keep your mouth natural with the tougue touching the upper palate. Avoid clenching your teeth or gazing out with an angry look. Keep your sacrum straight and slightly tucked under. If not, your spine will be affected, and your spirit will not be able to rise.

二、含胸拔背
Sink the Chest and Raise the Back

含胸者，胸略內含，使氣沉於丹田也。胸忌挺出，挺出則氣擁胸際，上重下輕，腳跟易於浮起。拔背者，氣貼於背也，能含胸則自能拔背，能拔背則能力由脊發，所向無敵也。

There should be a slight drawing in of the chest which allows the chi to sind to the Dan Tian. Avoid protruding the chest as this will cause the chi to rise which will lead to top heaviness, and the soles of the feet to float.

Raising the back means that the chi adheres to the back. If you can sink your chest, your back will naturally rise. If you can raise your back, your power will come from your spine enabling you to overcome any Opponent.

Sink the chest and raise the back are similar to when a cat is in readiness to launch an attack on its prey.

三、鬆　腰
Relax the Waist

腰為一身之主宰，能鬆腰然後兩足有力，下盤穩固，虛實變化皆由腰轉動，故曰：「命意源頭在腰隙。」有不得力必於腰腿求之也。

The waist is the commander of the body. If the waist is relaxed and loosened, the foundation, that is, your legs will be stable enabling you to issue power. Changes in solid and empty derive from the moving of the waist. It is said that「the waist is the well spring of your vital energy」. If you lack power in your movements, look for the weakness in your waist and legs.

四、分虛實
Distinguishing Solid and Empty

太極拳術，以分虛實為第一義，如全身皆坐在右腿，則右腿為實，左腿為虛；全身皆坐在左腿，則左腿為實，右腿為虛。虛實能分，而後轉動輕靈，毫不費力；如不能分，則邁步重滯，自立不穩，而易為人所牽動。

Distinguishing principle of Tai Chi. If your body centre rests in your right leg, then your right leg is solid, and your left leg is empty. If your body centre rests in your left leg, then your left leg is solid, and your right leg is empty. When you can clearly make this distinction, your movements will be light, agile, and effortless. If not, your steps will be heavy and chumsy, and you are easily unbalanced, due to the instability of your stance.

The philosophy of Yin Yang is the underlying principle of change in stepping.

五、沉肩墜肘
Sink the Shoulders and Elbows

沉肩者，肩鬆開下垂也。若不能鬆垂，兩肩端起，則氣亦隨之而上，全身皆不得力矣。墜肘者，肘往下鬆墜之意，肘若懸起，則肩不能沉，放人不遠，近於外家之斷勁矣。

The shoulders should relax and hang downwards. If the shoulders are raised, then the chi rises, and the whole body cannot summon up its power.

The elbows must relax and point downwardsl. If the elbows are raised, the shoulders will become tense inhibiting your ability to discharge you opponent to any great distance. Raising the elbows or shoulders is similar to breaking the jin which occurs in the external martial art systems.

六、用意不用力
Use the Mind and not Brute Force

太極拳論云：此全是用意不用力。練太極拳全身鬆開，不使有分毫之拙勁，以留滯於筋骨血脈之間以自縛束，然後能輕靈變化，圓轉自如。或疑不用力何以能長力？

蓋人身之有經絡，如地之有溝洫，溝洫不塞而水行，經絡不閉則氣通。如渾身僵勁滿經絡，氣血停滯，轉動不

靈，牽一髮而全身動矣。若不用力而用意，意之所至，氣即至焉，如是氣血流注，日日貫輸，周流全身，無時停滯。久久練習，則得真正內勁，即太極拳論中所云：「極柔軟，然後極堅剛也。」

太極拳功夫純熟之人，臂膊如綿裹鐵，分量極沉；練外家拳者，用力則顯有力，不用力時，則甚輕浮，可見其力乃外勁浮面之勁也。不用意而用力，最易引動，不足尚也。

According to the Tai Chi Classics, you use the mind and not brute force, In practice, your whole body is relaxed; not even using an ounce of brute force. If you employ brute force, you restrict the flow of energy through your sinews, bones and blood vessels. This will inhibit your freedom of movement preventing you from achieving agility, sensitivity, aliveness, circularity, and naturalness.

「How can you have power without using brute force?」By making use of the meridians in the body. {Meridians are a network of pathways which transport chi throughout the body. They connect the superficial, interior, upper and lower portions of the human body, making the body an organic whole. } The meridians are similar to the rivers and streams of the earth. If the rivers are open, then the water flows freely. If the meridians are open, then the chi flows. If the meridians are blocked as a result of using stiff force, then the circulation of chi and blood becomes sluggish. Hence, your movements will not be nimble, and even if a hair is pulled, your whole body will be in a state of disorder.

Although your abdomen is full and alive, there is no force being used. For the chi to sink down to the Dan Tian slowly and naturally, the mind needs to be relaxed. By deeply relaxing while preforming your Tai Chi movements, your chi will move freely to every part of your body.

This will benefit the body greatly. On the other hand, if you tense your mind and forcefully try to move your chi, or use unnatural methods to circulate the chi, is if more than likely that blockages will occur which are harmful to your health.

When you are able to use your mind and not brute force, then wherever your mind goes, your chi follows. After a long period of diligent practic and chi circulating freely everyday, you develop jin {an internal power which is different form hard force}. This is what the Tai Chi Classice means by 「from true softness comes true hardness」. The arms of one who has Tai Chi kung fu will feel extremely heavy; like steel wrapped in cotton. People who practise external martial art systems look strong when they exert hard force. However, when they are not bringing their hard force into use, they are light and floating. You can see that this merely a superficial kind of strength. Instead of using the mind, they use brute force, Which makes them easy to manipulate. Hence not worthy of praise.

七、上下相隨
Coordinate your Upper and Lower Body

上下相隨者，即太極拳論中所云：「其根在腳，發於腿，主宰於腰，形於手指，由腳而腿而腰，總須完整一氣也。」手動、腰動、足動、眼神亦隨之動，如是方可謂之上下相隨，有一不動，即散亂也。

According to the Tai Chi Classics, 「the root is in the feet; issued through the legs; controlled by the waist; and expressed through the fingers. From the feet through the legs to the waist forms one harmonious chi」. When the hands, waist, and feet move, your gaze needs to follow in unison. This is what in meant by harmony of the upper and lower body. If one part of the body is not in concordance with the rest, it will result in chaos.

When you first learn Tai Chi, your movements are larger and more open than those of a seasoned practitioner. The larger movements ensure that you waist and legs are moving in concordance, and all parts of the body are in harmony.

八、內外相合
Unify your Internal and External

太極拳所練在神，故云：「神為主帥，身為軀使。」精神能提得起，自然舉動輕靈。架子不外虛實開合。所謂開者，不但手足開，心意也與之俱開，所謂合者，不但手足合，心意亦於之俱合，能內外合為一氣，則渾然無間矣。

Tal Chi trains the spirit. It is said that「the spirit is the leader, and the body follows its command」. If you can lift your spirit, then your movements will naturally be agile and alive. Postures are nothing more than solid and empty, opening and closing. Opening does not just involve the hands and feet, but they must work in concordance with the opening of the heart/mind. Closing does not just concern the hands and feet, but they should coordinate with the closing of the heart/mind as well. When the internal and external are unified as one harmonious chi, then there are no gaps anywhere.

The heart/spirit is like a concealed sword. Form the outside, your practice has the appearance of being relaxed and comfortable, but on the inside, your heart/spirit is concentrated and sharp as a sword.

九、相連不斷
Continuity; no Stopping

外家拳術，其勁乃後天之拙勁，故有起有止，有續有斷，舊力已盡，新力未生，此時最易為人所乘。太極拳用意不用力，自始至終，綿綿不斷，周而復始，循環無窮。原論所謂「如長江大河，滔滔不絕」，又曰「運勁如抽絲」，皆言其貫串一氣也。

The external martial art systems employ brute force which is stiff and unnatural. This force stops and starts; moves in a jerky fashion. When the old force is finished before the new one has begun, this is the time when one is most vulnerable to attacks. In Tai Chi, you use the mind and not brute force. From the beginning to the end, the movements are continuous without stopping; like an endless circle. This is what the Classics means by 「a great river flowingcontinuously never ending」, or 「moving the jin like reeling silk from a cocoon」. The above conveys the idea of stringing the movements together into one harmonious chi.

If your movements stop and start, you will be easily taken advantage of by your opponent because you have exhausted your old strength, and the new power is not yet born.

十、動中求靜
Seek Serenity in Activity

外家拳術，以跳躍為能，用盡氣力，故練習之後，無

不喘氣者。太極拳以靜御動，雖動猶靜，故練架子愈慢愈好。慢則呼吸深長，氣沉丹田，自無血脈僨張之弊。學者細心體會，庶可得其意焉。

The external martial art systems consider leaping and crouching to be of value. They exhaust their energy and after practice, they are out of breath. Tai Chi uses serenity to counter activity. Even when you are moving, you remain tranquil. When practising the posturse, the slower you move, the better the result. Slowness enables your breath to become deep and long with the chi sinking to the Dan Tian. This will naturally prevent the pulse rate from elevating. Students of Tai Chi should think deeply on the above in order to grasp its meaning.

It is important to practise the movements slowly, so that you can understand the meaning within the movements. Practising slowly helps to regulate your breathing enabling your breath to become deep and long allowing your chi to sink to the Dan Tian. Practising in this manner also preventy the fault of top heaviness which is caused by the chi rising up.

-Narrated by Yang Cheng Fu-Recorded by Chen Wei Ming-Expanded upon by Fu Sheng Yuan.

陳微明爲永年太極拳社成立 10 週年賀詞

A Message to Commemorate the 10th Anniversary of the Yong Nian Tai Chi Association

陳微明
（Chen Wei Ming）

Mr. Fu Zhong Wen of Yong Nian has received the teaching and guidance from his relative, Mr. Yang Cheng Fu. Mr. Fu has learnt accurately to a very high standard, and has made no alterations, which is why people say that his Tai Chi is authentic.

Mr. Fu founded the Yong Nian Tai Chi Association（in 1944）, and has spread the art to the public for no charge. Ten Years have now passed since the founding of the Association, and I would like to say a few words to commemorate the occasion, When it comes to continuing the legacy of Yang Style Tai Chi, who else is there to compare with Fu Zhong Wen?

Chen Wei Ming was the first tuti（disciple）of the Great Master Yang Cheng Fu. He was a well known scholar, and he was responsible for his, teacher going to shanghai. Different from a student, a tuti（disciple）is accepted into the Yang family through formal ceremony, and is entitled to receive the full transmisson of the art. Disciple in this context has no religious connotation.

傅君鍾文永年　楊澄甫師之晚威得

師之傳授規矩準繩絲毫不爽故人

蔣為太極拳之正宗劍蔣永年太極

孝社教授學者不取報酬成就甚眾

今屆十載屬余書數語以為紀念爰

楊先大舍　鍾文其誰歟　陳微明

傅鍾文題永年太極拳社社訓

The Yong Family Tai Chi Chuan Motto

Master Fu Sheng Yuan emphasizes the importance of, the four principles of Zhin, Hen, Li, Zhen in the development of Tai Chi Chuan.

'Zhin' – Diligence

Hard work and effort is a prerequisite for skilled development. Daily practice on a regular basis will ultimately be rewarded by beneficial results.

'Hen' – Perseverance

It is important that a long enduring sense of purpose should be cultivated. A sense of purpose combined with regular daily practice serve to achieve that purpose.

'Li' – Respect

Respect for your master, teacher and fellow man is paramount. Deal with others taking into consideratioin their backgrounds and in the light of their expectctions. Mutual respect serves to enhance a sense of community in a society where individuals must treat each other with respect.

'Zhen' – Sincerity

Sincerity in attitude or motivation is a pre–requisite for learning Tai Chi Quan. In order to achieve, a genuine resolve to pursue your goal must exist. Deal with others sincerely if you wish them to reciprocate. Maintain sincerity in the fore of your dealings with others and you will achieve a smooth flow in relationships.

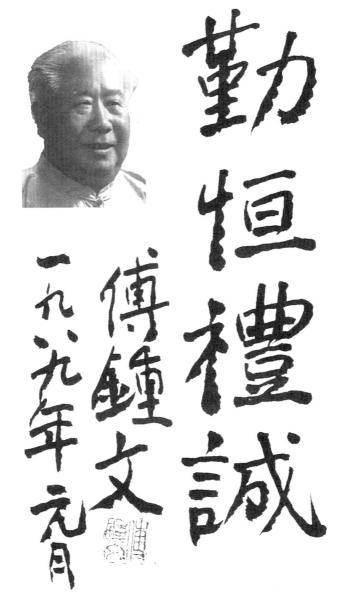

勤恒禮誠

傅鍾文

一九九年元月

Calligraphy by Grandmaster Fu Zhong Wen

楊家太極拳的練法及要點

太極拳源遠流長，太極文化始於《易經》，其內涵博大精深，是我國傳統哲學與武術、醫術和導引術完美的結合。天地為一大太極，人身為一小太極，故人欲鍛鍊身體，先練太極拳為宜，太極拳之動作以腹為主，不動則矣，動則全身皆動，腹既為人全身最中處，腹部一動，兩腰、兩手、兩足皆不疾而速。太極拳動作之發動以腹（即丹田）為主，不用劇烈之力，全身之動作無有不到，外面極其柔和，內裡延綿不斷之力，息息增長。

學練楊氏太極拳，首先要理解「鬆」、「固」、「凝」三字訣：何為鬆，體要鬆；何為固，氣要固；何為凝，氣要凝。體鬆、氣固、神凝，漸漸可以達到太極之境界，但其所以然之故，必學拳者學到某種程度方能自我體會。

（一）體要鬆

「鬆」字淺顯的解釋，就是不用力（不用強力）。蓋一用力，動作即不能自然。著意在用力之部分，則其他各部分必不平均。不用強力，動作自然，周身普傳，動作無所不到，而且平均如一。而鬆不等於空。勉強用力是硬的，所謂拙力。拙力雖大，是一部分的力，而不得其中。不用力是柔的，所謂沉勁。沉勁雖輕而小，是全部的力，能得其中。

（二）氣要固

「固」字淺顯的解釋，就是不散漫，體鬆而氣固。體雖不用力而氣卻不散漫。氣不散漫，動作始能不散漫，動

作不散漫，周身始能一體。如何能使氣固，即把氣壓在腹部，不要浮在上面，但與深呼吸盡量擴大肺部，將橫隔膜壓抑下去不同。練拳之時，肩要垂，肘要墜，腰要塌，久而久之，氣自然沉下，所謂心虛腹實是也。腹實則氣固，身體便有重心，無論手足如何動作，重心總在腹，得其重心，動作自如矣。故曰氣固則身自穩也。

（三）神要凝

「凝」字淺顯的解釋，就是內外相合，而能凝定也，體鬆、氣固矣。內外不相合，絕不能心之所到，即身之所到，惟內外相合，然後身心一氣。所謂內外相合，肩與膀合，肘與膝合，手與足合，是謂外三合；心與意合，意與氣合，氣與力合，是謂內三合。內外相合是謂六合，六合則身體中正矣。身體中正，神即提得起。

太極拳的動作剛柔相濟，連綿不斷，鬆沉自然，精神內固，呼吸自然等要點，皆要與實踐相結合，我父提出的永年太極拳社社訓「勤、恆、禮、誠」，就是要求學員練拳要勤學苦練，持之以恆，以禮服人，以誠相待。只有堅持刻苦習練，年復一年，在老師的親授和個人的努力下，才能掌握正確的練功方法，不斷提高技藝。同時還要懂得太極拳每個動作的要領和用法，細心研究揣摩。太極拳蓋不離掤、捋、擠、按、採、挒、肘、靠八法，進、退、顧、盼、定五行也。太極拳法，以心行氣，不用拙力，純任自然，蓋太極練功，沉肩墜肘，氣沉丹田，以氣周流全身，意到氣至。練到此地位，其力不可限量，此不用拙力純以神行，功效顯著。先師云：極柔軟然後極堅剛，蓋此意也。

楊家太極拳精練 28 式動作名稱

1. 起　勢
2. 攬雀尾
3. 單　鞭
4. 提手上勢
5. 白鶴亮翅
6. 摟膝拗步
7. 手揮琵琶
8. 肘底捶
9. 倒攆猴
10. 高探馬
11. 右分腳、左蹬腳
12. 左右打虎式
13. 雲　手
14. 玉女穿梭
15. 野馬分鬃
16. 指襠捶
17. 上步攬雀尾
18. 單　鞭
19. 下　勢
20. 金雞獨立
21. 上步七星
22. 退步跨虎
23. 轉身擺蓮
24. 彎弓射虎
25. 進步搬攔捶
26. 如封似閉
27. 十字手
28. 收　勢

Introduction

Form 1　Opening Form（Tai Chi Qi Shi）
Form 2　Grasping The Peacock's Tai（Lan Que Wei）
Form 3　Single Whip（Dan Bian）
Form 4　Raise Hands（Ti Shou Shang Shi）
Form 5　White Crane Spread Its Wings（Bai He Liang Chi）
Form 6　Left Knee Brush（Lou Qi Ao Bu）
Form 7　Hands Strumming the Lute（Shou Hui Pi Pa）

楊氏太極拳精練28式動作名稱

一、起勢（1-3圖）

一、起 勢

1. 兩臂徐徐向前向上，高至肩平，手掌略側，掌心斜向下。

2. 兩臂以肘領手慢慢向下，落於胯側前，兩腕微坐。

【要點】：

兩臂關節要鬆，尤要精神內固，氣沉丹田，鬆肩墜肘，兩掌心應微向裡，腋窩處要留有餘地，不能夾緊。

Stand upright and naturally in a relaxed position, with your feet a shoulder width apart and toes pointing forward. Arms should hang narurally with your shoulders and elbows relaxed. Keep your head upright, eyes gazing straight ahead. Keep your whole relaxed.

Raise both hands with palms facing the floor, until the hands

reach the shoulder level with the fingers pointing forward. Allow your elbows to sink. The bending of your elbows facilitates the bending of your wrists. Push down and back with the palms. Sick your hands to the hips, ensuring that fingers point forward and palms face the floor.

Point to note

• Your Chest should not protrude and Chi should sink to the Dan Tian. Attempt to relaxed the body totally.

• Your weight should be evenly distributed on both feet.

• The body axis should be upright and erect in a naturally and comfortable posture.

• Keep your mind alert and concentrated, but in a tranquil state.

• While pressing down, elbows should point to the floor, recede and sink.

• The upper arms should not be pressed agianst the body. While the hands are being moved, keep the body axis aligned and steady.

4　　5

二、攬雀尾（4-8 圖）

二、攬雀尾

左掤：

1. 右腳轉腳跟，腳尖外撇約 50 度，同時兩手抬起與腰平，向右轉體，重心坐於右腳。兩手隨腰向右側将帶，然後左手在前，右手相隨，左臂向前向上掤，右手與左臂相合，左腿抬起向左側（南方）邁步成左弓步，胸向南。

2. 左腳跟抬起向右呈 45 度，同時腰向右轉，兩手分開，右手下採到略高於胯，掌心向下，胸向西，眼前向（西）平視。

右掤：左腿坐實不動，抬右腿向右前方邁步，左手同時略向後畫一小弧；右手繞腹部弧形向前掤出，兩手相合，左手與右手腕相疊，成右掤。重心在右腿，成右弓

捋　　　6

步。

　　捋：兩臂同時向左前畫弧，右掌心向下，左掌心向上，兩手後捋，重心坐於左腳。

　　擠：兩手掌心同時相對變轉，左手疊於右腕，左手拇指在右腕下部，重心前移，向前擠出成右弓步。

　　按：

　　1.右手翻掌，兩手由交叉打開，掌心向下，左上右下。

　　2.分掌與肩同寬，重心後移，同時兩手後移坐腕，腰微左轉，重心坐於右腳。

　　3.雙手向前相合按出，掌心斜相對，指尖向上，重心同時前移成右弓步。

　　【要點】：

　　攬雀尾是太極拳體用兼全的總手。上、下肢體動作要

擠 7

協調一致。在虛實變化中，要保持鬆腰，收臀，尾閭中正。

2a. Ward Off Movements

(i) Left Ward Off

• Turn clockwise 45° On your right heel, transferring weight to the turning foot. The body should also turn 45°. At the same time, bend your right knee and sink on your right leg. Bend your left knee and lift foot. Use your waist to circle both hands clockwise. Raise your left leg when palms face each other as if holding a ball. Keep your right hand uppermost, palm facing the floor. Step out on your left heel off center to the left. Slowly palms, moving the hands diagonally. The weight should now be fully transferred to the left foot which should be positioned half your foot length behind the right.

On completion of the move your right foot should be pointed straight ahead with the left foot at 45 Keep your left hand level with

your left shoulder and your arm rounded. The right palm should be two hand widths away from your waist and facing the floor. Again, the arm should be rounded and your weight on your left foot.

(ii) Right Ward Off

• Raise your right foot, draw it towards the left and draw your right palm across the front of the body, the palm moving in a circular scoping manner. The left palm should face the floor and circle in an anticlock wise fashion until both palms face each other as if holding a ball. During this movement your waist should be moving anticlockwise.

2b. Roll Back Movements

• Place the right heel forward in a bow stance and as the waist unwinds clockwise, the right hand should move diagonally across the front of the body with the back of the hand leading and palm inclined towards the ceiling. The left palm follows, facing the floor. The hands do not touch at the wrist, but are naturally close to each other. The eyes look forward and body faces straight ahead. Right foot points forward and the left foot, which is as the rear of the bow, remain angled at 45°.

三、單　鞭

三、單　鞭

由前勢重心不變，右腿轉腳跟，腳尖內扣成 45 度，兩掌略沉，隨腰左轉畫弧，再右轉畫弧。然後右手變勾，左手掌心向裡置右腕內側。同時左腿抬起向左前方邁步，兩臂打開，左手徐徐翻掌向前按出，掌心斜向前方，成左弓步，右腿自然伸直。左膝與腳尖垂直。眼向前平視。

【要點】：
兩臂畫弧要以腰帶動。扣腳時重心保持在右腿不變。

<3> Start with your weight on the right leg, standing in a right bow stance. Turn anticlockwise on the right heel through 135°

maintaining your weight on the turning foot. At the same time, turn your waist. Sit down on the right leg, as both hands circle anticlockwise in an elliptical shape. Keep your palms inclined down wards slightly, but not parallel to the floor. Continue to draw the hands in an anticlockwise movement until the arms move out the tip of the thumb. The left palm faces the middle of the chest. Mean–while, the left foot is withdrawn. With your waist turning to the left, the left leg is placed forward coming down on the left heel. The left palm is drawn anticlockwise in a circle motion. The eyes follow the movements and direction of the left hand. Turn the left wrist so that the left palm sits upright on the wrist and faces away from the body at a slight angle. The body weight should be transferred to the left in concert.

Point to note

 • When drawing the arms in elliptical fashion, the motion must be generated from the waist.

 • With right hook hand the shoulders should be relaxed and the elbow pointing to be floot.

 • All movements should occur at the same height.

41

四、提手上勢

四、提手上勢

由前勢重心不變，左腿轉腳跟內扣30度，右腿抬起向正前方邁出，腳跟貼地，腳尖微抬。兩手同時向下沉，再相合向前向上，掌心相對。右手在前、在上，左手在右肘內側。重心在左腿。眼向前視。

【要點】：
提手上勢是一合勁，腳與手的動作要協調一致，兩足不能在一條直線上。

10

4. Raise Hands

<4> With your weight on the left leg, turn your foot clockwise on the left heel in slightly. The right leg is raised slightly and placed on the floor resting on the heel, keeping the knee slightly bent. At the same time, the right hook is opened and the arms open slightly, then the hands come together in a closing movement, right hand higher than the left. The left hand moves towards the right elbow, palm facing the floor obliquely. Gaze straight ahead at eye level, but angling the body slightly to your left. Sit on the left leg. Ensuring that the right knee is not locked, but slightly bent.

Point to note

• Keep your weight on your left leg to ensure the flow of movement.

• Avoid, slouching your shoulders or pushing your chest forward.

五、白鶴亮翅

五、白鶴亮翅

抬右腳向前落步，腳尖內扣45度，同時兩手隨腰微向左轉相合，左手在上，右手在下，手心相對。重心右移到右腳，左腿抬起向前邁出，腳尖貼地，腳跟微抬。同時右手隨腰轉向上架起，變轉掌心向前，左手向左下採，落至左胯側，坐腕，目平視前方。

<5> With your weight on the left leg, draw the right leg back. At the same time draw both hands together as if holding a ball to your left; right hand scooping and left hand circling inwards to the body, while the waistmoves slightly to the left. Step out with the right heel, with the toe turned in and transfer your weight to the right foot, pivoting on the heel. After transferring the weight to the right, lift the left leg

11

5. White Crane Spread Its Wings

and touch the floor with the toes facing forward. Separate the palms, like a crane unfurling it's wings on the heel. After transferring the weight to the right, lift the left leg and touch the floor with the toes facing forward. Separate the palms, like a crane unfurling it's wings. Your weight should be on the right leg, while your left toe should be touching the floor with the heel off the floor.

Points to note

● Differentiate between the solid and hollow leg in order to achieve a smooth, slow transfer of weight.

● The waist should rotate around the axis of the lower spine, moving the four limbs.

● The right palm is held forward in a slanting position above and forward of the temple and should not be cupped. Refrain from holding the palm horizontally and keep your elbow pointing down.

六、左摟膝拗步

六、左摟膝拗步

右手內旋下落，從腰部向後、向上弧形撩起，再弧形回轉從耳旁經過向前推出，掌心斜向前。左手畫弧向上向右到右胸前，掌心向下，然後再弧形向左前繞膝摟過，坐腕落於左胯旁。同時，左腿向左前邁出，成弓步，右腿自然伸直，重心在左腿。

【要點】：
眼神要隨右掌轉換，身體保持中正，整個動作要協調，圓滿，柔和。

12

6. Left Knee Brush

<6> Lower your right palm, circle it anticlockwise up to the height of your ear, then push forward with the hand inclined inwards slightly and sitting upright on the wrist. Move your left hand to the right of your body, palm facing the floor and ascending slightly above waist level. At the same time, sit down on your right leg lifting slightly. Step forward, while your left hand brushes past the knee in a horse shoe–like shape. The brushing hand descends as it moves out.

Point to note
- When stepping forward on the left leg, gently lower the heel in a controlled manner.
- When turning the waist, your body axis must remain upright and should not lean or sway.
- The right leg must be firm and steady, while the waist remains relaxed.

七、手揮琵琶

七、手揮琵琶

抬右腿前跟半步，左腿抬起然後腳跟著地，腳尖微抬成左虛步。同時，右掌隨轉腰向後向下，左手向前向上翻掌。右掌心斜向上，左掌心斜向下，兩掌相合。

【要點】：

手隨腰動，虛實分清。

7. Hands Strumming the Lute

<7> Shifting your weight to your left leg, lift the right foot. Ensuring that the foot is placed at 45°, sit down naturally on the right leg, Shift all the weight back to the right leg. Raise your left, and place it in front of you with the heel down. At the same time, while raising the left hand, draw the right hand back moving it to the inside of the left elbow with the palm inclined towards your body.

Points to note
● It is vital to differentiate between the solid and empty leg. The raising and lowering of the legs must be done in a light and gentle manner. Avoid double weighting.
● Avoid swaying and leaning.

49

八、肘底捶

八、肘底捶

右手向後弧形撩起，左手向右到右胸前，掌心向裡成掤式，左腳抬起向前，腳跟落地，兩手隨腰向左轉動，弧形繞圈。右手向左至前方正中握拳向下壓至左臂肘底，左手從右手內側向前伸出，掌心斜向前；右手握拳在左肘下方，重心坐於右腿。

【要點】：

兩手隨腰向左轉動時距離不變，左掌不能平放或下蕩，定式時必須坐腕豎立。

<8>While sitting on the right leg, turn your waist clockwise and circle your right hand anticlockwise up to ear height, with the palm

14

8. Fist Under Elbow

facing away and sitting upright on the wrist. At the same time, move your left hand to your right to adopt a warding off position with palm facing the body. Turn your waist anticlockwise and shift your weight to the left foot, then move the right foot naturally forward and sit back on the right foot, toes touching first, As the right wrist comes in line with the center of the body, begin to form a first with the right hand then draw the first towards your body. As the right hand is drawn towards the body, move the weight back to the right leg and continue circling the left palm anticlockwise over the right arm using the elbow to move the palm. Raise the left leg and rest on the left heel with the toes off the floor. Continue to withdraw the first until the eye of the first aligns below the left elbow. The left hand should sit upright on the wrist and the palm should be inclined to the right.

Points to note

• Make sure your body is facing 45°.

九、倒攆猴（15-16圖）

九、倒攆猴

1. **左倒攆猴：**右手變掌經腹前，弧形向後撩於肩高，手心斜向上。左臂外旋，兩臂對開。同時左腿向後退一步，腳尖先落地，重心後移。右手回轉由耳旁經過向前推出，掌心斜向前。左手弧形向後向下抽回於左胯旁，掌心向上。整體動作隨腰左轉，面向前方，眼向前平視。

2. **右倒攆猴：**動作相同，方向相反。

【要點】：

退步時兩腳應有一個橫向距離，不可踩在同一條直線上。

<9> (i) With your weight on the right leg, turn your waist clockwise. At the same time circle your right hand backwards, with

15 16

9. Step Back to Repulse the Monkey

the palm facing and the left arm extended slightly, palms facing downward. At the same time, lift the left leg and step back off center, the left foot coming down toe first. Transfer your weight back to the left leg, pushing the right hand forward past the ear, while pulling the left hand back to come to rest at the left hip. Sit on the left leg with the right heel down. Pivot your right foot on the heel with the toe slightly off the floor, as the right leg relaxes. Your body should be inclined at a slight angle to the left and does not face straight ahead. Your right palm should be in line with your chest sitting on the wrist.

(ii) Sitting on your left leg, circle your left hand back, palm facing forward. Lift the right leg & step back off center, toe first, and transfer the weight back. At the same time complete the movement with the left palm pushing forward and the right pulling back to the hip & turning the palm up.

Points to note
• Keep shoulders level when performing the opposing movement.

53

十、高探馬

十、高探馬

右手弧形後撩，回轉由耳旁經過，俯側掌向前探出。左手外旋向後向下弧形收於左腹側，掌心向上。重心在右腳，左腳尖虛點地面，兩腿自然站直。

【要點】：
右手前探和左手後收與右腿直立要協調。

<10> Turn your waist clockwise and circle your right hand b ackwards with palms facing forwards. As your raise your body on the rear leg and draw the left leg in by turning your waist slightly anticlockwise. Your right foot is the solid foot and the left is hollow.

17

10. Pat The High Horse

Touch the floor with the ball of the left foot. At the same time, turn the left palm anticlockwise to incline upwards, while retracting it to the waist. The right hand is brought in towards the ear and with fingers relaxing and palm facing the floor. The right hand moves to strike with the outer edge of the palm. Avoid straightening the right arm.

Points to note
- Sit firmly on the right leg and utilize the waist rotation to draw the leg in rather than the knee.
- As your right arm moves forward, relax your shoulder, instead, allow it to sink slightly. Your arm should remain rounded and elbow facing down.
- The striking edge of the right palm is formed by pulling the thumb edge of the hand towards the body and flexing the wrist.

十一、右分腳（18-19 圖）

十一、右分腳、左蹬腿

1. 右腿微坐，左腿抬起向左前邁步成弓步，同時兩掌相對交叉畫弧，面向右前方。右掌在前掌心斜向下。左掌心斜向上與右掌相對，置於右肘旁。

2. 左手隨腰向左，繞一小圈；右手弧形向左前與左手相合。然後提右腿向右前方分出，同時兩手左右分開，左腿站起，成右分腳。

3. 左腿下蹲，收右腿然後向右前邁步，成弓步。兩手交叉畫弧，轉向左前，左手在前掌心朝下，右手掌心向上在左肘旁。

4. 右手向右經胸繞一小圈，左手弧形向右與右手合於胸前，左手在外。然後提左腿向左前蹬出，同時兩手分

十一、左蹬腳（20-21 圖）

開，右腿站立，成左蹬腳。

【要點】：
分腳腳面自然繃平，力在腳尖，分腳與分掌要一致。
蹬腳腳尖應上翹，力在腳跟。方向在左前方。

<11> Sink on your right leg while lifting your left leg. Step out the left foot, heel first, into the left bow stance at 45°. At the same time, with your right hand uppermost, circle palm down in a clockwise motion, moving firstly towards and then away from the body to the right. Your left palm faces upwards and describes a circle in a clockwise motion. Your body should end up facing 45° to the right with your right palm facing obliquely. Follow the movements of your eyes. Draw the right hand down in a clock wise motion and scoop upwards looking 90° to

the left, while you cross the palms with the right forearm outside the left. Raise your right leg. Use the waist and turn to the right, while separating the hands with the palms facing outwards, and raising on the left leg to kick with the right toe. Right toe kick.

Sink on your left leg. Step out, 45° to your right and form a right bow stance. The hands describe circles anticlockwise, with the left hand uppermost and palm facing the floor. Yourright hand should be underneath, palm facing the ceiling. Transfer weight to the right and turn your waist 90° to the right, crossing left forearm outside the right. Turn and look to your left, while separating the hands with palms facing outwards and rising on the right leg to kick with the left heel. Your eyes should be following the movements of the left hand.

Points to note

• The outside hand of the cross always corresponds to the kicking leg.

• When kicking with your toe, your toes should be pointing downward. When kicking with your heels, your toes should be pointing upwards.

十二、左右打虎式（22-23 圖)

十二、左右打虎式

1. 由前勢右腿屈膝，左腿收回後向左前邁步，腳跟先著落。同時左手向右，掌心向上，置於右臂旁，右手掌心向下，兩手相合。重心前移成左弓步，兩手隨腰轉向左畫弧，右臂屈肘橫置於胸前握拳，左臂自下向上畫弧置於左額前握拳。兩拳眼上下斜相對。

【要點】：
兩掌在到位時才握拳，膝到拳到。

2. 左足尖裡扣，左腿坐實，抬右腿，身體右轉。同時，兩拳變掌，左掌略沉，掌心朝下，右臂外旋，掌心向上。右腿向前邁出，腿跟先落，身體繼續右轉，重心前移

成右弓步。兩掌同時向右畫弧，右手向右向上畫弧，握拳置於右額前，左手屈肘橫臂於胸前握拳。眼向前平視。

【要點】：

抬腳要充分，轉腰、變掌、提腳要協調一致。

<12> (i) Side to the Left to Tame the Tiger

Sitting on the right leg and draw your left hand back toward the right into a ward off position at the same time the right elbow drops and the right hand sits cocked on the wrist. Then step out into a left bow stance, left heel first at 45°, while moving your left arm across to the right of your body, palm inclined upwards. Your right hand is drawn back towards the body by dropping the right elbow. Your right palm should face downward, inclined away from the body. As you step forward on the left heel, the left and right arms move across to the left of the body, left palm rotating to sit palm up, generated by the waist movement. The left arm circles upwards above the left temple, while your right hand forms a first in front of your sternum.

(ii) Sidle to the Right to Tame the Tiger

With your weight on the left leg, turn 90° Clockwise on the left heel. Raise your right leg and draw it towards the body. Your waist should turn slightly to the right. Open your fists and sink firmly on the left leg, before stepping out right heel first at 90° to the right transferring your weight to the right foot and assuming a right bow stance. As your waist turns to the right, the arms are withdrawn in a motion similar to the 'Roll Back', from the left of the body to the right. The right hand moves up to form a fist, slightly above your right temple. The left hand moves to the center of the body, and forms a fist in front of the sternum.

Points to note

- The fists are formed at the completion of the move.

- The eye of the left fist faces the chin and is angled towards the body. The right elbows should point downward.

- The eye of the fist should face your right temple, with the eye inclined downward.

- Your gaze should follow the direction of your hands synchronous with your waist movement.

十三、雲　手（24-26圖）

十三、雲 手

　　重心左移，兩手變掌，右掌向右、向下畫弧，左手同時向上、向左畫弧。掌心朝裡。兩掌不停，收右腳向左落步於左腳側面，腳尖先落。左手隨腰弧形向左運行，逐漸翻掌向下。右掌自右下經腹前向左弧形運動，逐漸掌心向裡運到近左腕。右腳落實，腰向右轉，右掌隨腰自左下向上向右弧形運轉，左掌自左上弧形向下向右運轉。抬左腳向左橫向邁側步，腳尖先落地。右腳隨抬起向左跟進，腳尖先落地，兩手隨左、右轉腰向外畫弧。

　　【要點】：
　　兩腳距離約肩寬。兩手畫弧應隨腰轉。

25

<13> Transfer your weight to the left leg. Open your left hand and move your left arm outwards slightly in an anticlockwise circular motion. At the same time, your right hand opens out from the fist and moves down in a clockwise circular motion scooping across the front of the hips. At the same time, lift your right knee and bring your right foot down, toe first, shoulder width from the left, in a parallel stance. Your right hand continues to ascend in a circular motion as the left hand pushed down, then across the front of the hip in a scooping motion, using the waist to generate the move. Your weight should now be on the right leg. Lifting your left knee and step to your left, toe down first, while your right hand descends and moves across the front of the hips in a scooping motion, as your left hand ascends and moves across in front of your body. As the left hand sinks, the right palm should rise. Step to the left with your right foot, coming down toe first and transfer your weight to your right leg.

Points to note

● Your hand movements are driven by the waist.

● The stance should be neither too wide nor too narrow, with your toes pointing forward.

● Avoid double weighing and ensure that weight transfer coincide with the foot movements.

● Avoid straightening your arms, keep then rounded and your movements circular.

● Relax your shoulder and ensure your palms face inward.

十四、玉女穿梭 (27-28 圖)

十四、玉女穿梭

1. 兩掌腹前相合，左下右上掌心向上，然後左腳向左前邁步，重心前移成弓步，同時兩手對拉，左手向外、向前、向上翻掌架於額前，掌心向外；右手翻掌向前按出，掌心斜向前。

2. 轉左腳跟，兩手相合，左手在上，右手在下，身向後轉，重心回坐於左腳，隨即右腳抬起向右前邁出，兩掌對拉，重心前移成弓步，右手翻掌向上架於額前，左手翻掌前按。

【要點】：

扣腳充分，轉體 180 度，方向是兩斜角。

<14> Lift the knee and step out on the left heel, one full step diagonally to your left at 45° to assume a left bow stance at. Swing your left palm away from the body in an arc, first descending and then ascending, while the left palms initially faces towards you. As the hand raise to the top, allow your palm to turn clockwise and face outwards. Meanwhile, turn your right wrist anticlockwise until the palm inclines towards the floor, withdraw slightly and push forward. Your left palm should be just above your forehead, the palm facing outward, while your right palm should be in front of the body, hand sitting upright on the wrist at the center line of the body. If necessary, pivot on your rear foot, pushing the heel out to correct the bow stance.

Turn clockwise on you weighted left heel. Try to turn as far past 90° as possible. At the same time, turn your right hand and allow your left arm to come down in an arc. With the palm turning towards you, so that both hands face the body with your left palm on the inside, but not touching. Step out on your heel and assume a right bow stance as your waist turns clockwise. Lift your left heel slightly and pivot on you left toe. The arms separate with your right hand moving away from your body in an upward arc, palm turning in an anticlockwise fashion, until it faces forward. At the same time, your left palm turns clockwise with your thumb towards the body and moves forward to push.

Points to note

- Gaze beyond the pushing hands at eyes level into the distance.

十五、野馬分鬃（29-30 圖）

十五、野馬分鬃

1. 左野馬分鬃：

提左腳向前邁步。同時，左掌外旋下落，兩掌相合掌心相對，右掌在前在上，左掌在後在下。重心前移成弓步，兩手對分。左手向前，向側弧形分開。右手向下弧形分開，掌心向下，坐腕。

2. 右野馬分鬃：

左腳跟外轉 45 度，收右腿，同時兩手隨腰向左轉在腹前相合，左手在上掌心向下，右手在下掌心向上。然後邁右腿，重心前移成右弓步，腰向右轉，右手向右前上方，向側弧形分開；左手向左後下方弧形分開，掌心向下，坐腕。

【要點】：

分掌與轉腰要配合協調，分掌時手的路線是向前而不向外。

<15> Lift your left knee, allowing the foot to move towards you. Lower your right arm with the palm facing the floor and turn your left palm anticlockwise, finishing with wrists facing each other as if holding a ball to the right of the body. Sink on the right leg and place the left heel forward, to assume a left bow stance. At the same time, separate the palm. Your left palm moves forward in a straight line and towards the end of the movement, arcs across to the left of the body. Your right palm moves in the opposite the direction and should stop not far from the waist, palm facing the floor. Follow the direction of the waist and your right hand with your eyes. On completion of the move, gaze forward into the distance.

Pivot on the left heel turning clockwise to 45°. Follow a similar movement to the Left Parting The Wild Horse's Mane, except that your left palm faces the floor and the right palm will face upwards on the left side of the body when holding the ball. The strike palm will be the right rather than the left and step forward to assume a right bow stance.

Points to note
* The toes of the leading foot in the bow stance should be pointing straight ahead.

十六、指襠捶

十六、指襠捶

　　右腳外擺45度，左腳至右腳旁，同時左手向右畫弧，右手俯掌向下向後畫弧至腰部變拳。

　　然後左腿向左前方邁出，重心前移成弓步，左手繞膝前弧形摟至左側，右手向前沖出，拳眼向上。

　　【要點】：
　　左腿要低坐，左手摟膝與右掌前擊要同時進行。

<16> Turning clockwise 45° on your right heel. Transfer your weight leg and lift the left knee. At the same time, circle your right hand clockwise, with the palm facing the floor. Your left arm moves clockwise across your body. Sit down on the right leg and step forward on the left heel to adopt a left bow stance. Meanwhile, continue the circling motion of your hands to your right forming a fist with the right hand at the right hip. As you transfer your weight forward, move the right fist in a low forward punch, the fist rising naturally at the conclusion of the punch. Your left palm should be facing the floor and as you punch with the right, the left hand brushed past the left knee.

Points to note

• Your right punch must be synchronized with the transfer of the weight forward onto the left leg.

十七、上步攬雀尾（32-36圖）

十七、上步攬雀尾

左腳轉腳跟腳尖外擺 45 度踏實，右手變掌，兩臂打開，提右腿。然後邁右腿，重心前移成弓步。同時兩手上下抄合於胸前向右前上方掤去，兩臂呈弧形。

其他各式與前第二式攬雀尾同。

<17> With your weight on your left leg, turn on the left heel anticlockwise to 45°. At the same time, separate your palms, with the left palm inclined diagonally up and the right palm down. Step forward in a right bow stance in order to Ward Off to the right. Roll Back, Press and Push. Refer to description of Form 2.

十八、單　鞭

十八、單　鞭

同第三勢。

十九、下　勢

　　右腳跟轉，腳尖外撇 45 度，坐右腿，左腿伸直成仆步，左手墜肘向後收，屈肘經胸側弧形而下，從左腿裡側前穿。眼看左手方向。

　　【要點】：
　　左臂回收要大於 90 度，不可過屈，並與下蹲要一致。

十九、下 勢

<19> From a left bow stance, turn clockwise on your right heel through 90°, sinking on your right leg into a very low stance. At the same time your left hand draw back with your elbow pointing to the floor and finger pointing straight ahead. Your right arm moves backwards with the body, with the fingers remaining in the hook. As you sit back, draw your left hand towards the body, sinking it in a circular motion. As you move forward, your left hand continues circling then starts to rise upwards.

Points to notes

• Avoid leaning forward or looking down at the floor and don't allow your posterior or chest to protrude.

• Your waist is use to retract the left hand.

• The thigh must not touch the right calf when sinking down.

二十、金雞獨立（39-40 圖）

二十、金雞獨立

1. 左式，重心前移，左腳尖外撇 45 度，右腿提起成左獨立式，右手變掌經右腿旁向前、向上挑起，右肘右膝相對，左掌同時弧形下摟到左胯旁，坐腕。

2. 右式，左腿屈膝下蹲，右腳向後距左腳一腳距離落下，重心漸漸移向右腿，左腳屈膝提起。同時右掌弧形下落於胯前上方，掌斜向下。左掌自下向前、向上隨提左膝弧形挑起，掌心斜向前呈側掌，坐腕。

【要點】：
挑掌與提膝要一致。

40

<20> While transferring the weight forward, keep the body low and turn on the left heel 45° anticlockwise. Your left hand draws back to sit on the wrist next to the left hip, with fingers pointing forward and the palm facing the floor. At the same time, lift the right knee together with the right hand until the knee is slightly higher then the hip, and toe inclined naturally towards the floor. On completion of the right hand movement, the palm sits on the wrist with the finger tips pointing upwards and elbow over the thigh. Sink on the left leg while dropping your right knee until your right foot is 45° and that your step back diagonally to the right of and behind the left foot. Sit down firmly on your right leg until you are stable. Then repeat Golden Cock stance by standing on the right leg & lifting your left knee.

Points to note
• When rising avoid dragging the rear foot continuously or lifting it off the floor too abruptly.

二十一、上步七星

二十一、上步七星

　　左腳向前落實，右腳向前腳尖點地成虛步。右手握拳向前上方於左掌相交於胸前。左手握拳兩手同時向前推擋，左拳在上，右拳在下，重心在左腿。

　　【要點】：
　　兩手先合再同時向前推擋。

<21> Lower your left leg and place your foot forward onto the heal at 45°. At the same time lower your left arm forward with palm facing down, as you bring your right hand up to form a fist. The eye of the fist should face upwards. Move your right leg forward to form a false leg with the toe pointing towards the floor. The right fist continues its upwards advance on the outside of the left, until hand and fist cross, with the right fist on the outside of the cross. The left hand retracts slightly as the right fist moves forward and as then cross together, the left hand forms a fist and both fits move forward in unison.

Points to note

• Maintain your weight on your left leg, with the right toe pointing towards the floor.

二十二、退步跨虎

二十二、退步跨虎

右腿後撤一步，腳尖先落踏實，左腳抬起，以腳尖點地，成左虛步，重心在右腿，同時兩拳變掌分開，右掌向右上，掌心向前，左掌向左下，掌心向下，坐腕。

【要點】：
撤步時腰向右轉，成虛步時再回轉。

<22> Move your right leg back, coming down toe first and transferring your weight backwards, ensuring that your foot is 45°. At the same time, your waist turns in a clockwise motion to the right. The first move clock wise with the waist and separate whilst the leading foot lifts and comes down again on the left toe. Your fists open out into palms which continue their circling movement. The palms move apart and your left palm finished facing the floor and the right should be sitting upright and facing forwards.

Points to note
• The separation of the palms at the finished should be wider than white crane spreads wings

二十三、轉身擺蓮（43-46 圖）

二十三、轉身擺蓮

1. 左掌弧形上護至左額前，右掌弧形而下經胸前推出。

2. 右掌微抬，左掌微落，兩掌掌心向下，隨右腳為軸向後轉體，左腳腳跟向左後側面落地，兩掌弧形擺向右側面，重心在右腿。

3. 重心移向左腿，右腿向左提起向右擺蓮，兩掌向左依次擊打右腳面，兩手隨勢擺到左前斜方。

【要點】：

轉身要穩，擺踢要腳迎手，手擊腳，互相迎擊。

<23> Circle the left hand in a clockwise movement upwards, with the palm facing out, towards the front of the forehead. At the same

time, circle the right hand clockwise towards the body and push forward, while sinking on the right leg.

Using your waist to initiate the movement, start turning clockwise on your right toe, maintaining your weight on the right leg. Continue turning on the toes ensuring that the weight is maintained on the ball of your right foot. At the same time, the left hand moves down until your right palm is slightly higher than your left with both palms facing the floor. The waist circles through 360°, finishing the move with the right toe pointing forward and the left foot coming down on the heel at 45°. The hands continue to your right, finishing with the right hand slightly lower than the left, and both palms facing downward. Your weight should still be on the right leg. As you transfer weight to the left, lift the right knee and circle the right foot in a clockwise motion towards the palms. At the same time, move your palms in an clockwise motion towards the toe. Your foot moves from left to right and the palms move from right to left in a sweeping motion making contract with the top of the foot. The hands come to rest to the left of you, palms facing down.

二十四、彎弓射虎

二十四、彎弓射虎

　　左腿屈膝坐實，右足向右斜方邁出成弓步，兩掌隨腰向右弧形變彎弓射虎，右掌向右向上，握拳於太陽穴旁，左掌握拳向左前方弧形沖擊，拳眼斜向上。

【要點】：
兩手畫弧、隨腰轉動。

<24> Sink on your left leg while stepping out on the right heel to adopt a right bow stance at 45°. Your right palm should be facing the ceiling and your left palm facing the floor. Use the waist to generate the motion which is similar to that of Taming the Tiger to the right. Continue the circling movement of the right hand, causing it to ascend in a circling motion to the right temple. The left hand moves outwards and forms a fist, knuckles pointing out wards. The eye of the right fist should be inclined downward and the eye of the left fist inclined upwards.

Points to note
- Make sure the elbow is facing down.
- Your eye must follow the movement of the left fist.

二十五、進步搬攔捶

二十五、進步搬攔捶

重心移向左腿，左拳變掌，右拳隨左掌弧形向下回帶。提右腳邁出，重心移向右腿，右拳向右搬出，左掌相隨扶助，然後提左腿向前邁出，拳掌前後相對分開。重心向前變弓步，右拳向前沖出，拳眼向上。左掌向後附於右臂內。

【要點】：
連續邁步時要邁步如貓行，上下相隨。

<25> Transfer your weight back to the left leg and move the right fist down and across to the left of the waist. At the same time, the left

fist opens and draws back to finish behind the right. Lift the right foot of the floor to step out on the heel at 45°, while circling your waist clockwise, and transferring your weight to the right leg. Lift the left leg and draw the right fist back to the side of the waist, as the left palm pushed forward with the finger tips pointing upwards. Step forward into a left bow stance. Draw the left arm back and punch forward with your right fist. Your waist should circle anticlockwise slightly when punching. As your right fist drives forward, your left palm draws back in a reciprocating motion to finish close to the inside of the right elbow.

Points to note

• Your fist should be at waist level with the eye of the fist facing upwards.

• When punching forward, twist the fist anticlockwise until the eye of the fist is facing upwards.

二十六、如封似閉

二十六、如封似閉

　　重心移向右腿，左掌從右臂下貼臂向前，右拳變掌，腰略向左轉，兩掌分開，掌心向內，兩掌蓄勢，翻掌即按，重心向前成弓步。

【要點】：
兩手不可先向後再向前按，是分掌後翻掌即按。

<26> Transfer your weight to the right leg, taking care not to lift your left toe off the floor as you sit back. Slide your left hand under the right elbow with the palm facing down. Relax your right fist and turn your left palm anticlockwise as both palms separate and fan outwards.

Withdraw the hands separating them at shoulder–width apart. Ensure that both palms finish facing forwards, with the hands sitting upright on the wrist. Your palms should not face straight ahead, but should be turned inwards slightly towards each other. Push forward, moving into a bow stance and your right leg should straighten naturally, without locking the knee.

Points to note
• Make sure the hands are not pulled too closely towards the body after separating the palms.

二十七、十字手（50-51 圖）

二十七、十字手

　　左足尖裡扣 90 度，身向右轉，坐實左腿。同時兩掌隨轉腰屈肘向右移動到額前，掌心向前。然後兩手分開，弧形向下再轉向上相抱於胸前，掌心向裡。同時收右腳於左腳側落地，身體緩緩站起，兩臂向上與肩高。

　　【要點】：
　　兩臂始終弧形，不可僵直。

51

<27> Turn clockwise on your left heel through 90°, keeping your weight on the left leg. Lift your right leg and placing the right foot down, toe first, so that you assume a squatting position with your feet at shoulder width. Lift yourself up with the right leg. At the same time, turn your body clockwise keeping your hands in line with the center of the body, then raise and separate them in a circular motion, pushing down, scooping and then crossing with the right arm outside the left. As the legs completely straighten, the hands are crossed with palms facing you.

Points to note
- Avoid being double weighted.
- Relax the shoulder and arms must be rounded.

二十八、收 勢

二十八、收 勢

　　兩手前伸翻掌，左掌心貼右掌背，手心向下，兩掌分開與肩平。兩臂以肘帶手漸漸向下，兩手坐腕落於胯兩側。指尖自然下垂。

<28> Turn the right palm anticlockwise and the left palm clockwise to face the floor. Retract the elbows and allow the palms to sink, sitting on the wrists. Relax the hands and let them drop.

93

跋 一

傅聲遠師父風塵僕僕馬不停蹄地在世界各地推廣嫡傳楊氏太極拳，百忙中不忘著書立說，近期內又將出版拳、劍、刀等系列著作，完整地保存了楊澄甫先師傳傅鍾文老師系的太極拳、械風格內容。這是師父繼《嫡傳楊式太極拳教練法》出版後再接再厲的嘔心之作。在這之前，師父已經出版多本中英文拳著及錄影帶、光碟等教材，暢銷世界各地，可謂著作等身。

由於他數十年如一日在國內外推廣傳統楊氏太極拳，功勞巨大，因此榮獲中國武協頒發的武術推廣獎，也獲得中國武術院頒發的武術段位八段。

師父9歲從永年到上海隨其父傅鍾文習練楊家太極拳，耳濡目染、勤勞苦學，全面繼承了楊澄甫先師太極拳晚期定型的85式楊氏太極拳架及器械。他早年跟隨父親傅鍾文在上海同濟大學、華工學院、財經學院及國內各地教拳。

1988年定居澳洲柏斯，並創立世界永年太極拳聯盟及傅聲遠國際太極學院。他以澳洲爲大本營，向歐美及南洋一帶傳藝，桃李滿天下，將楊氏太極拳傳播到世界各地。傅鍾文太師是近代中國楊氏太極拳的代表人物之一，全面繼承了楊澄甫先師晚期定型的太極拳，經年累月，一絲不苟，被其師兄著名太極拳名家陳微明贊譽爲太極拳正宗。

陳微明是楊澄甫先師器重的弟子，德高望重，影響深遠的博學之士，著有《太極拳術》等書，是研究楊氏太極拳的必讀著作。他在1954年上海永年太極拳社慶祝10周年紀

念時，親筆寫下這樣的贊語：「傅君鍾文永年楊澄甫師之晚戚，得師之傳授，規矩準繩絲毫不爽，故人稱太極拳之正宗——發揚光大，捨鍾文其誰子耶。」在武林慣例中，師弟能獲得師兄的公開贊許和勉勵是非常罕見的，也是一件不容易的事。因此傅鍾文太師傳承的太極拳風格，是楊氏太拳愛好者學習的典範。

楊澄甫先師晚期在《太極拳使用法》和《太極拳體用全書第一集》中刊登的拳照，渾厚圓滿，舒展大方，氣魄大，形象美，達到爐火純青的境界，是楊式太極拳的楷模，經典拳架。可惜的是，拳照中缺乏轉折過渡的動作。因此，習者莫不師從傅鍾文太師、傅聲遠大師、傅清泉師兄傅家三代尋求這些細膩重要的運作過程，以求合乎正宗。這是因為在楊澄甫的弟子中，最相似楊澄甫定型的太極拳者，當推傅鍾文太師。

傅鍾文太師早年編著的《楊氏太極拳》、《楊氏太極刀》，被譯成多國文字，早已成為楊氏太極拳的重要著作。1989 年由上海同濟大學出版的傅鍾文、傅聲遠編著《楊氏太極教練法》一書，出版後即洛陽紙貴。

1990 年傅聲遠師父編著的《嫡傳楊氏太極拳教練法》，用的是師兄清泉的拳照。清泉師兄有"太極少帥"之美譽，秉承家學，長期隨爺爺及父親身邊，親受教誨。曾在中國國內獲得楊式太極劍冠軍、中國武術七段，目前是少壯派的太極拳名師，學生遍布中國、日本、澳洲等地。該書已接二連三再版，仍供不應求。

師父傅聲遠 9 歲隨父練拳，苦下功夫，深受其父影響，他秉承家訓，在國內及海外走南闖北，應邀到世界各地授

拳。他虛懷若谷，不爭名利，教學認眞，在上海曾受聘於同濟大學、華工學院、財經學院、職工大學等高校教授太極拳。1986年他挾藝南來，先後在澳洲、泰國、新加坡、馬來西亞等國教授太極拳。定居澳洲柏斯後，他每年都風塵僕僕多次赴歐美四十多個國家授拳訪問，深受太極拳愛好者的歡迎，桃李滿天下，可謂是東南亞等國傳播楊式太極拳85式定型拳的第一人。如今傅聲遠師父的《嫡傳楊家太極拳》、《嫡傳楊家太極劍》、《嫡傳楊家太極刀》，即將出版，全面地展現了楊澄甫先師的拳、械體系，相信太極拳愛好者可以由傅師父的完整系列著作，得到啓發，登堂入室地直探楊公澄甫定型太極拳、械眞髓。

是爲跋

受業：黃建成

2006年6月23日馬來西亞光華日報　柔佛辦事處

註：作者爲馬來西亞中文報資深報人及文化人、馬來西亞柔佛新山永年太極拳學會會長、馬來西亞武術網和馬來西亞太極網絡站長。

Postscript I

Master Fu Shengyuan promotes Yang Style Taijiquan in the world without a stop, and writes books at the same time. Recently, the series books including boxing, sword and knife are on publish, which completely preserved, boxing and weapon contents of Master Fu Zhongwen (Yang Chengfu's disciples) . This is another masterpiece after his publication of Exercise Method of Direct-Line Yang Style Taijiquan. Before that, master Fu has published many boxing writings, video tapes and CDs in Chinese and Engilsh, which sold briskly and easily all over the world.

For his persistent promotion on traditional Yang Style Taijiquan both in domestic and abroad for decades on end, he is granted Wushu Promotion Award by Chinese Wushu Association, and gained Wushu Level 8 from Chinese Wushu Academy. From Yongnian to Shanghai, Master Fu exercised Yang Style Taijiquan following his father Fu Zhongwen since 9 years old, through assiduously exercise, he completely inherited 85 FormYang Style Taijiquan and weapons from Master Yang Chengfu. In his early years, he followed his father Fu Zhongwen to taech Taijiquan at Shanghai Tongji University, Shanghai University of Economics and Finance, South China University of Technology and other domestic places.

The master settled down at Perth, Australia in 1988, and creatde World Yongnian Taijiquan Association and Fu Shengyuan International Taiji School. Based in Australia, he taught many disciples and students Taijiquan at Europe, USA and Southeast Asia, spread Taijiquan all over the World. Master Fu Zhongwen, Fu Shenguan's teacher and father, is one of representatives of Yang Style Taijiquan in modern times, has completely inherited definitized Taijiquan from master Yang Chengfu, and was highly praised by his senior fellow apprentice Chen Weiming, the famous Taijiquan expert, as orthodox Taijiquan. Chen Weiming is thought highly of by deceased teacher Yang Chengfu, is an erudite commendable person who has writings of Taijiquan and others. In 1954, Chen Weiming autographed the following words of praise: "Fu Zhongwen is satisfying purple of Yongnian Yang Chengfu, have proper behavior, and is known as orthodox Taijiquan. Fu Zhongwen will further develop and promote Taijiquan". In the Wulin convention, it is seldom that junior fellow apprentice is publicly praised by senior fellow apprentice. The style of Taijiquan from Fu Zhongwen is paragon to Yang Style Taijiquan lover. The photo of master yang Chengfu in Taijiquan Exercise Method and Entire Book on Taijiquan (No.1) shows his decent boxing posture, but it is a pity that there miss the transition posture in the photo. The person who know what's what all try to find the importnt orthodox postures from three generations of Fu Zhongwen, Fu Shengyuan and Fu Qingquan, this is because that in the Yang Chengfu's disciples, the most similar Taijiquan posture type should be Fu Zhongwen. The Yang Style Taijiquan and Yang Style Taijidao (taiji knife) which written by Fu Zhongwen at his early age has been branlated into many languages and be look as important writing for Yang Style Taijiquan. The Exercise Method of Yang Style Taijiquan, which written by Fu Zhongwen and Fu Shengyang, was published by Shanghai TongJi University Press in 1989. After the publication, the book was sold in overwhelming popularity. The book used boxing photo of Fu Zhongwen. But it is a pity that the paper quality of the book is not good. In 1990, Yongnian Yang Style Taijiquan (written by Fu Shengyuan) is published by Malaysia Yongnian Taijiquan Association. About 600 Master Fu Shengyuan's photo are used in the book, the book was already sold out, domestic lovers hasn't chance to get the book. Shanghai TongJi University published Exercise Method of Direct-Line Yang Style Taijiquan written by Fu's three generations in 2000, the book adopt Fu Qingquan's Boxing Picture. Fu Qingquan has good reputation of "junior commander in chief of Taijiquan". He followed his father and grandfather and received paternal teaching for long time, has gained champion of Yang Style Taijiquan (taiji sword), China Wushu Level 7, Now he is a famous Taijiquan master wit lots of disciples all over China, Japan, Australian, and other places. The book was republished for many times, but the damand still exceeds supply.

Master Fu Shengyuan practiced Taijiquan since 9 years old, deeply influenced by his father.he is extremely open-minded, stand aloof from the worldly affairs, and conscientiously teach Taijiquan at Tongji University, Shanghai University of Economics and Finance, South China University of Teachnology, College for Workers & Staff and other universities in Shanghai. In 1986, he went to south, taugh Taijiquan at Australia, Thailand, Singapore, Malaysia and other countries. After he teach Taijiquan each year, is popular with Taijiquan lovers. He can be No.1 who teach and transmit 85 Form Yang Style Taijiquan at Southeast Asia with student all over the world. At present, the 3 books of Proficiency in 28 Postures of Yang Style Taijiquan, Yang Style TaijiJian (taiji sword), Yang Style Taijidao (taiji knife), will be published in succession. These books will fully exhibit Taijiquan and weapons system of master Yang Chengfu. I believe the Taijiquan lovers will take a hint in studying the essence of Yang Chengfu Style Taijiquan and weapons through the complete series books. The Postscript is given hereby.

Student: Huang Jiancheng
Jun. 23, 2,
Note: the author is senior journalist and literator of Chinese newspaper in Malaysia, president of Johore Bahru Yongnian Taijiquan Association, Webmater of Malaysia Wushu website and Malaysia Taiji website. 006 at Johore Office, Kwong Wah Yit Poh & Penag Sin Poe

嫡傳楊家太極拳——精練28式

99

跋 二

　　吾師傅聲遠是一代太極宗師傅公鍾文之獨子，楊家太極拳親族傳人，中國武術八段，世界永年太極拳聯盟主席、澳洲傅聲遠國際太極拳學院主席。1931 年生於河北永年廣府，9 歲赴上海隨父習練楊家太極拳。吾師年幼聰穎，在其父的嚴格訓練下，無間寒暑、刻苦磨練，少年時打下了堅實的基礎，解放前在其父創辦的永年太極拳社積極協助推廣楊家太極拳。

　　建國後，任上海體育學院武術教練，20 世紀 60 年代初被聘爲武術裁判，多次擔任市級、國家級武術裁判工作；70 年代曾受聘於上海同濟大學、化工學院、財經學院等大學，教授楊氏太極拳；1984 年與其父參加武漢國際太極拳邀請賽，表演了傳統楊式太極拳、劍、刀、杆（槍），受到了大會的熱烈歡迎和贊賞，新華社記者於上海新民晚報特刊《父子太極》以贊揚。吾師傅聲遠助父義務傳授楊式太極拳數十年，門徒尤重，成就斐然。他先後受聘擔任上海永年太極拳社顧問、上海精武體育總會名譽理事、深圳太極拳研究會顧問、珠海太極拳協會顧問、淮南永年太極拳社名譽社長、邯鄲太極拳友會名譽會長、泰國太極拳會顧問、新加坡楊氏太極拳健康中心顧問總教練、日本東京太極拳社名譽社長、西班牙太極拳學會名譽會長、葡萄牙太極拳學會總教練、印度太極拳學會名譽會長等。

　　1986 年，應澳洲友人盛邀移居澳洲，爲傳正宗楊式太極拳於海外，同時遠赴英國、法國、德國、美國、比利時、

瑞士、西班牙、葡萄牙、波蘭、智利、捷克、巴西、紐西蘭、阿根廷、馬西來亞、新加坡、日本、泰國等四十多個國家傳播楊氏太極拳，爲楊氏太極拳傳播海外和人類的健康做出了一定貢獻。1990 年，澳洲前總理霍克在柏斯接見並宴請了傅氏父子，贊揚其爲澳洲人民健康做出了貢獻。

吾師傅聲遠，敦厚穩重、樸實無華、虛懷若谷，太極拳造詣頗深，在國內外武術界享有崇高威望，其拳架純正，沉穩中帶有輕靈，拳、劍、刀、杆（槍）、推手無靡不精，大有其父之風範。時令吾師已 76 歲，秉承父訓，仍不遺餘力，傳正宗楊氏太極拳於海內外。

吾師著有英文版《嫡傳楊家太極拳》、《嫡傳楊家太極劍》，中文英文版《楊氏太極拳精練二十八式》、《二十八式輪椅太極拳》，中文版《嫡傳楊氏太極拳教練法》等著作。此次出版《嫡傳楊家太極拳》、《嫡傳楊家太極劍》、《嫡傳楊家太極刀》，書中圖照分別攝於 2003 年和 2006 年，圖照清晰，架式純正，動作規範，詳解拳理拳法，通俗易懂，是一部難得的傳統楊氏太極拳資料，堪稱當今學習楊氏太極拳之範本。受師父之示，爲本書寫跋，弟子受寵若驚，倍感吾師之器重。然本人才疏學淺，草草數語難盡書中之精奧，謹以段文代爲跋。

傅聲遠弟子 楊清波 2006 年 6 月於古趙邯鄲

Postscript II

My teacher Fu Shengyuan is the only son of Fu Zhongwen (master of Taijiquan) , Cognation descendant of Yang Style Taijiquan, China Wushu level 8, chairman of World Yongnian Taijiquan Union, chairman of Australia Fu Shengyuan International Taijiquan Institute. He was born in 1931 at Guangfu, Yongnian, Hebei, has went to Shanghai and exercised Taijiquan followed his father since 9 years old. Under stric training from his father, my teacher got a firm base. He actively promoted Yang Style Taijiquan at Yongnian Taijiquan League before liberation.

After PRC established, He held the post of Wushu Coach at Shanghai Physical Training School; at beginning of 60's, he was engaged as Wushu referee, and has atcted as municipality-level, state-level Wushu referee for many times; in the 70's, he was engaged to teach Taijiquan at Shanghai Tongji University, Shanghai University of Economics and Finance, South China University of Technology and other universities; in 1984, in company with his father, he took part in Wuhan International Taijiquan Invitation Competition, and performed traditional Yang Style Taijiquan, Jian (sword) , Dao (knift) , Gan (pole) with his father,was warmly welcomed by the organizer and audience, Xinmin Evening Newspaper has published "Taiji father & Son" to praise them. My teacher has helped his father volunteered to teach Yang Style Taijiquan for decade years, taught lots of disciples, gained great achievements. He has successively acted adviser of Shanghai Yongnian Taijiquan League; honor director of Shanghai Jingwu Gym General Society; adviser of Shenzhen Taiji Research Society; adviser of Zhuhai Taijiquan Association; honor president of Huainan Yongnian Taijiquan Association; honor chief of Handan

Taijiquan Lover Association; adviser of Thailand Taijiquan Association; adviser and chief coach of Singapore Yang Style Taijiquan Healthy Center; Honor president of Japan Tokyo Taijiquan Society; honor president of Spain Taijiquan Association ; chief coach of Portugal Taijiquan Association, honor president of India Taijiquan Association and others. In year 1986, invited by Australian friend, for teaching authentic Yang Style Taijiquan to overseas, he went aborad to teach boxing. In 1988, his whole family settled down at Perth, Australia. He and his father established Wushu Hall to widely teach disciple Yang Style Taijiquan, and went to England, France, Germany, America, Belgium, Switzerland, Spain, Portugal, Poland, Chile, Czechoslovakia, Brazil, New Zealand, Argentina, Malaysia, Singapore, Japan, Thailand, altogether more than 40 countries to spread Yang Style Taijiquan, made certain contribution to people's health. In 1990, Australian Former Prime Ministe Mr. Bob Hawke gave an interview to Fu Zhongwen and Fu Shengyuan, praised them for their contribution to health of Australian people.

My teacher Fu Shengyuan is honest and sincere, earnest and simple, extremely open-minded. He has high prestige in domestic and abroad Wushu groups; he is expert in Taijiquan（boxing）, Jian（sword）, Dao（knife）, Gan（pole）, Tuishou. His boxing posture is pure and authentic, combined calm with nimble together. Now my teacher has already 77 years old, he still obeyed orders from his father, spared no efforts to teach Yang Style Taijiquan at home and abroad. He has written English version Direct-Line Yang Style Taijiquan, Direct-Line Yang Style Taijiquan（sword）; Chinese and English version Proficiency in 28 Postures of Yang Style Taijiquan, Play 28 Postures of Taijiquan on Wheelchair and Chinese version Exercise Method of Direct-Line Yang Style Taijiquan. This time, he pulished proficiency in 28 Postures of Yang Style Taijiquan, Direct-Line Yang

Style Taijiquan（Sword）, Direct—Line Yang Style Taijidao（knife）（Color version in Chinese and English）, the photos in the books are took in 2003 and 2006. The book has clear photos, standard postures, detail explanation on boxing principle, easy to understand, is a rare information on traditional Yang Style Taijiquan, it can be exercising model for Yang Style Taijiquan. Been instructed to write the Postscipt by my teacher, I was surprised at the unexpected honor. So I tried my best to write down the postrcsipt hereby.

Writer: Disciple of Fu Shengyuan Yang Qingbo

Jun. 2006 at Handan

傅聲遠先生聯絡地址：

澳洲地址：813, ROWLEY ROAD, FORRESDALE, 6112, PERTH, W. Australia

澳洲電話：61-8-93970610　13901649686

上海地址：200081　上海市虹口區四達路58弄8號203

上海電話：（021）65751686

導引養生功

1 疏筋壯骨功+VCD 定價350元

2 導引保健功+VCD 定價350元

3 頤身九段錦+VCD 定價350元

4 九九還童功+VCD 定價350元

5 舒心平血功+VCD 定價350元

6 益氣養肺功+VCD 定價350元

7 養生太極扇+VCD 定價350元

8 養生太極棒+VCD 定價350元

9 導引養生形體詩韻+VCD 定價350元

10 四十九式經絡動功+VCD 定價350元

張廣德養生著作　每冊定價350元

全系列為彩色圖解附教學光碟

輕鬆學武術

1 二十四式太極拳+VCD 定價250元

2 四十二式太極拳+VCD 定價250元

3 八式十六式太極拳+VCD 定價250元

4 三十二式太極劍+VCD 定價280元

5 四十二式太極劍+VCD 定價250元

彩色圖解太極武術

1 太極功夫扇
定價220元

2 武當太極劍
定價220元

3 楊式太極劍
定價220元

4 楊式太極刀
定價220元

5 二十四式太極拳+VCD
定價350元

6 三十二式太極劍+VCD
定價350元

7 四十二式太極劍+VCD
定價350元

8 四十二式太極拳+VCD
定價350元

9 楊式十六式太極劍
定價350元

10 楊氏二十八式太極拳+VCD
定價350元

11 楊式太極拳四十式+VCD
定價350元

12 陳式太極拳五十六式+VCD
定價350元

13 吳式太極拳五十六式+VCD
定價350元

14 精簡陳式太極拳八式十六式
定價220元

15 精簡吳式太極拳三十八式拳架・推手
定價220元

16 夕陽美功夫扇
定價220元

17 綜合四十八式太極拳+VCD
定價350元

18 三十二式太極拳 四段
定價220元

19 楊式三十七式太極拳+VCD
定價350元

20 楊氏五十一式太極劍+VCD
定價350元

21 嫡傳楊家太極拳精練二十八式
定價220元

太極跤

1 太極防身術

定價300元

2 擒拿術

定價280元

3 中國式摔角

定價350元

簡化太極拳

1 陳式太極拳十三式

定價200元

2 楊式太極拳十三式

定價200元

3 吳式太極拳十三式

定價200元

4 武式太極拳十三式

定價200元

5 孫式太極拳十三式

定價200元

6 趙堡太極拳十三式

定價200元

原地太極拳

1 原地綜合太極二十四式

定價220元

2 原地活步太極四十二式

定價200元

3 原地簡化太極拳二十四式

定價200元

4 原地太極拳十二式

定價200元

5 原地青少年太極拳二十二式

定價220元

6 原地兒童太極拳十捶十六式

定價180元

健康加油站

1
糖尿病
預防與治療
定價200元

2
胃部機能與強健
胃部
Stomach
定價180元

3
不孕症治療
不孕症治療
定價200元

4
簡易醫學急救法
簡易醫學急救法
定價200元

5
肥胖健康診療
肥胖
健康診療
定價200元

6
肝功能
健康診療
定價200元

7
高血壓健康診療
高血壓
健康診療
定價200元

8
高血糖值健康診療
高血糖值
健康診療
定價200元

9
尿酸值健康診療
尿酸值
健康診療
定價200元

10
膽固醇中性脂肪健康診療
膽固醇
中性脂肪
健康診療
定價200元

11
痛風
劇痛消除法
定價180元

12
三溫暖健康法
三溫暖
健康法
定價180元

13
手・腳病理按摩
手腳
病理按摩
定價180元

14
B型肝炎預防與治療
B型肝炎
預防與治療
Health
定價180元

15
吃得更漂亮、健康
吃得更漂亮
健康
定價180元

16
茶使您更健康
定價180元

17
圖解常見疾病運動療法
圖解常見疾病
運動療法
定價180元

18
科學健身改變亞健康
科學健身改變亞健康
定價180元

19
簡易萬病自療保健
簡易萬病自療
保健
定價220元

20
王朝秘藥媚酒
王朝秘藥媚酒
定價180元

立見實效
保健操
定價180元

22
越吃越幸福
越吃越性福
定價200元

23
荷爾蒙與健康
荷爾蒙與健康
定價180元

運動精進叢書

1 怎樣跑得快

定價200元

2 怎樣投得遠

定價180元

3 怎樣跳得遠

定價180元

4 怎樣跳的高

定價180元

5 高爾夫揮桿原理

定價220元

6 網球技巧圖解

定價220元

7 排球技巧圖解

定價230元

8 沙灘排球技巧圖解

定價230元

9 撞球技巧圖解

定價230元

10 籃球技巧圖解

定價220元

11 足球技巧圖解

定價230元

12 羽毛球技巧圖解

定價220元

13 乒乓球技巧圖解

定價220元

14 曲線球與飛碟球

定價300元

15 街頭花式籃球

定價280元

16 精彩高爾夫

定價330元

17 巴西青少年足球訓練方法

定價230元

快樂健美站

柔力健身球
定價280元

2 自行車健康享瘦

定價280元

3 跑步鍛鍊走路減肥

定價280元

4 創造健康的肌力訓練

定價220元

5 舒適超級伸展體操

定價280元

6 水中有氧運動

定價280元

完美身材
定價280元

8 創造超級兒童

定價280元

9 使頭腦變聰明

定價280元

10 防止老化的身體改造訓練

定價280元

11 三個月塑身計畫

定價280元

12 懶人族瑜伽

定價280元

定價240元

14 忙裡偷閒練瑜伽祛病養生篇

定價240元

15 健身跑激發身體的潛能

定價200元

16 中華鐵球健身操

定價180元

17 彼拉提斯健身寶典

定價280元

18 全身保健操＋VCD

定價280元

瑜伽美姿美容
定價180元

20 豐胸做自信女人

定價200元

21 輕鬆瑜伽治百病

定價280元

22 瑜伽秀體小品

定價280元

常見病藥膳調養叢書

1 脂肪肝
脂肪肝四季飲食
定價200元

2 高血壓
高血壓四季飲食
定價200元

3 慢性腎炎
慢性腎炎四季飲食
定價200元

4 高脂血症
高脂血症四季飲食
定價200元

5 慢性胃炎
慢性胃炎四季飲食
定價200元

6 糖尿病
糖尿病四季飲食
定價20

7 癌症
癌症四季飲食
定價200元

8 痛風
痛風四季飲食
定價200元

9 肝炎
肝炎四季飲食
定價200元

10 肥胖症
肥胖症四季飲食
定價200元

11 膽囊炎、膽石症
膽囊炎、膽石症四季飲食
定價200元

傳統民俗療法

1 神奇刀療法
定價200元

2 神奇拍打療法
定價200元

3 神奇拔罐療法
定價200元

4 神奇艾灸療法
定價200元

5 神奇貼敷療法
定價200元

6 神奇薰洗療法
定價20

7 神奇耳穴療法
定價200元

8 神奇指針療法
定價200元

9 神奇藥酒療法
定價200元

10 神奇藥茶療法
定價200元

11 神奇推拿療法
定價200元

12 神奇止痛療法
定價2

13 神奇天然藥食物療法
定價200元

14 神奇新穴療法
定價200元

15 神奇小針刀療法
定價200元

16 神奇刮痧療法
定價200元

品冠文化出版社

推理文學經典巨著，中文版正式授權

名偵探明智小五郎與怪盜的挑戰與鬥智
名偵探柯南、金田一都讚嘆不已

日本推理小說鼻祖—江戶川亂步

1894年10月21日出生於日本三重縣名張〈現在的名張市〉。本名平井太郎。
就讀於早稻田大學時就曾經閱讀許多英、美的推理小說。
畢業之後曾經任職於貿易公司，也曾經擔任舊書商、新聞記者等各種工作。
1923年4月，在『新青年』中發表「二錢銅幣」。
筆名江戶川亂步是根據推理小說的始祖艾德嘉‧亞藍波而取的。
後來致力於創作許多推理小說。
1936年配合「少年俱樂部」的要求所寫的『怪盜二十面相』極受人歡迎，
陸續發表『少年偵探團』、『妖怪博士』共26集……等
適合少年、少女閱讀的作品。

1 ～ 3 集　定價300元　試閱特價189元